Jelly and Bean

Activities for books 17-24 in the B Digraphs Series

These **34** photocopiable activity sheets are to accompany books 17 - 24 in the **B Digraphs Series**.

The aims of the writing activities are to get children to:
1. think about what they have read,
2. respond to questions to show they have understood the text,
3. reinforce the new graphemes within the words in the stories,
4. learn the spellings of common exception words.

There are **4** activities for each book in these series. They cover the recognition of grapheme/phoneme correspondences, full word recognition, comprehension of specific sentences, comprehension of passages and of the whole story. Whilst carrying out the tasks, children are also practising their handwriting and assimilating new knowledge.

The consonant graphemes *'sh, ch, th, ng, ck'* and the vowel graphemes *'ee, ea, ay, ai, er, ir, or, y, oo, ou, ow'* are used within words in the vocabulary of the activities.

The common exception words *'he, she, they, come, all, her, goes, water, can't, move,* are introduced within the vocabulary of the story books. Other common exception words *'one, two, what, when, where, who, does, doing'* are introduced within the vocabulary of the activities.

Marlene Greenwood
December 2015

@ Jelly and Bean Ltd

Contents

17B
Activity 1	Write missing words in sentences	ship She splash
Activity 2	Write missing words in sentences	He Smash path
Activity 3	Match phrases and pictures	a water tub, Jelly jumps, Kevin jumps,
Activity 4	Answer comprehension questions	

18B
Activity 1	Write missing words in sentences	Crash feet sheep
Activity 2	Write missing words in sentences	three tree cross
Activity 3	Write missing words in sentences	coming tree sheep
Activity 4	Answer comprehension questions	

19B
Activity 1	Write missing words in sentences	Rain water out
Activity 2	Write missing words in sentences	raining puddle swim
Activity 3	Write missing words in sentences	rain sails tail
Activity 4	Answer comprehension questions	

20B
Activity 1	Write missing words in sentences	hay day hatch
Activity 2	Write missing consonant digraphs	sh ch th ck ng
Activity 3	Write the story	hay day laid hatch
Activity 4	Answer comprehension questions	

21B
Activity 1	Write missing words in sentences	rubbish egg-shells crust
Activity 2	Write missing words in sentences	fish chips goes sleep
Activity 3	Match words and pictures	apple peel, egg shells, banana skin,
Activity 4	Answer comprehension questions	

22B
Activity 1	Write missing words in sentences	look fluffy rush
Activity 2	Write missing words in sentences	creeps rush seven
Activity 3	Write the story	creeps rabbit fluffy past
Activity 4	Answer comprehension questions	

23B
Activity 1	Write missing words in sentences	long stick catch
Activity 2	Write missing words in sentences	string feels fishes
Activity 3	Write the story	stick catch fishing frogs
Activity 4	Answer comprehension questions	

24B
Activity 1	Write missing words in sentences	very chips quick
Activity 2	Write missing words in sentences	much feels sleep
Activity 3	Match rhyming words	bed red, cat hat, chips lips, dish wish,
Activity 4	Answer comprehension questions	

Name..

Write the correct word in each space.

| ship | She | splash |

Lotty sees a little .... in the water tub. She runs to the water tub. .... jumps in it. Splash, ..., splash! Lotty has fun with the ship in the tub.

Name..

Write the missing word in each space

| He | Smash | path |

Kevin jumps in the tub. .... hits the tub with his feet. Crack! Split!

......................! The tub splits. Water goes all over the .... Oh no! Kevin and Lotty are on top of the ship.

17 B activity 2

Name..

Draw a line from each phrase to the correct picture.

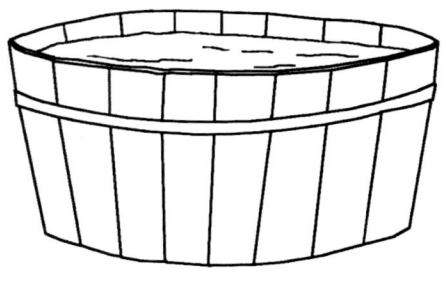

a water tub

Lotty jumps

Kevin jumps

a split tub

a ship in the tub

Name..

Write the answers to the questions on the dotted lines.

1. What does Lotty see in the tub?

....

2. Who jumps in the tub first?

....

3. What happens when Kevin jumps in the tub?

....

....

Name..

Use the words in the boxes to fill in the gaps in the sentences.

| very | sheep | feet |

Kevin comes speeding down the hill very fast. Bump! He hits a sheep with his .... He hits another .... Then he hits a third sheep. The sheep are .... cross with him.

Name..

Use the words in the boxes to fill in the gaps in the sentences.

three

tree

cross

Kevin hits .... sheep as he comes down the hill. They are very .... with him. They push him up against a .... 'Baa, baa, baa.' Oh no! Kevin can see Lotty coming down the hill very fast.

Name..

Write the correct word in each space.

coming

tree

sheep

Kevin can see Lotty .... down the hill very fast. Kevin jumps behind the .... Lotty crashes into the three sheep. Oh no! They are all in a heap under the tree. The .... are very, very cross.

Name..

Write the answers to the questions on the dotted lines.

1. Who does Kevin hit with his feet?

....

2. Are the sheep happy or cross with Kevin?

....

3. What happens when Lotty comes down the hill?

....

....

Name..

Write the correct word in each space.

Rain

water   out

.... is falling on the kennel.

Kevin and Wellington are in a puddle in the kennel. The .... gets deeper.

Kevin and Wellington have to swim to get .... of the deep water.

Name..

Write the correct word in each sentence.

1. It is .... on the kennel.

snowing

raining

swimming

2. The rain makes a big .... in the kennel.

puddle   apple   bubble

3. Kevin and Wellington have to swim to get out of the ....

water   today   play

19B activity 2

Photocopiable activities from Jelly and Bean

Name..

Write the correct word in each sentence.

1. The dogs wait in the kennel to stay out of the ....

rain pain main

2. The ship has seven ....

tails sails fails

3. Jelly looks at Wellington's................. .

jail tail nail

Name...

Write the answers to the questions on the dotted lines.

1. Is it a sunny day in this story?

....

2. Does the rain go into the kennel?

....

3. What do Kevin and Wellington do to get out of the water?

....

....

....

19B activity 4   Photocopiable activities from Jelly and Bean

Name..

Write the correct word in each space.

| hay | day | hatch |

The hen has laid two eggs on the

.... Every .... the cats and

the dogs go to see her. The eggs

.... after twenty-one days

and the hen has two chickens.

Name..

Write the correct letters in each word. .

| sh ch th ck ng |

fi......

si......

......icken

tru......

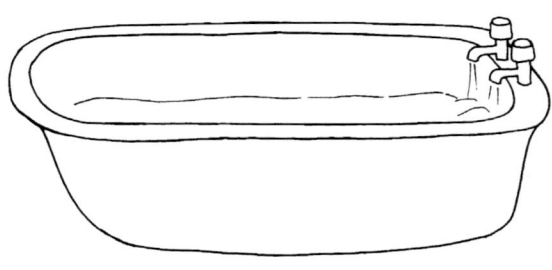

ba......

20B activity 2   Photocopiable activities from Jelly and Bean

Name..

Write a story about these pictures.

1	2	hay
3	4	laid
		day
		hatch

....

....

....

....

....

20B activity 3   Photocopiable activities from Jelly and Bean

Name..

Write the answers to the questions on the dotted lines.

1. How many eggs does the hen lay?

....

2. Who comes to see her every day?

....

....

3. What happens when the eggs crack?

....

....

Name..

Write the correct word in each space.

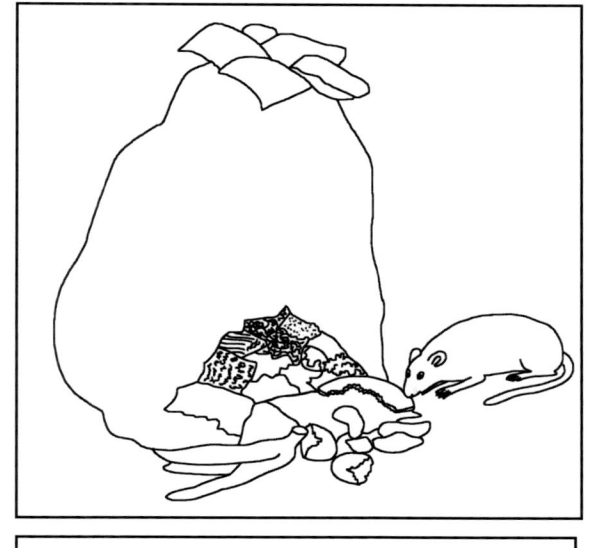

| rubbish |
| egg-shells |
| crust |

A rat has bitten a hole in a bag of .... The rat can see a banana skin, ..., crisps and a crust of pizza. The .... of pizza is not good to eat. .

Name..

Write the correct word in each sentence.

| fish | chips | goes | sleep |

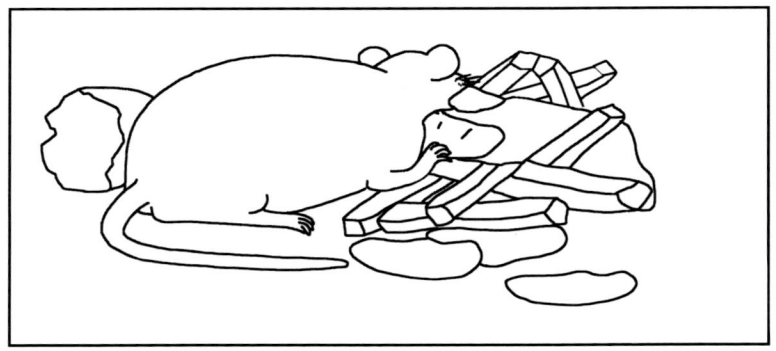 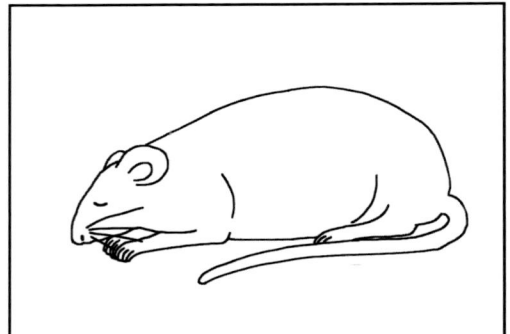

The rat can smell .... and .... in the bag of rubbish. Mmmm. The rat eats all the fish and chips. Mmmm. The rat is full. He .... back to his den. He has a long ....

Name..

Write the correct words next to each picture.

apple peel	egg shells
banana skin	pizza crust
	sandwich

....

....

....

....

21B activity 3   Photocopiable activities from Jelly and Bean

Name..

Write the answers to the questions on the dotted lines.

1. Does the rat eat all the rubbish?

....

2. What does he like to eat best?

....

3. Where does he go when he is full?

....

4. What does he do there?

....

....

21B activity 4

Photocopiable activities from Jelly and Bean

Name..

Write the correct word in each space.

| look | rush | fluffy |

Jelly sees a rabbit go into a hollow log. Jelly goes into the log to .... for it. She feels lots of .... things .... past her. Jelly goes back out of the log and onto the grass.

Name..

Write the correct word in each sentence.

1. Jelly .... into a hollow log.

creeps jeeps feeds

2. Lots of soft fluffy things .... past Jelly.

rush cash mash

3. Jelly sees a big rabbit on the grass. She has .... little rabbits.

six seven three

Name..

Write a story about these pictures.

creeps   rabbit

fluffy   past

....

....

....

....

....

22B activity 3   Photocopiable activities from Jelly and Bean

Name..

Write the answers to the questions on the dotted lines.

1. What does Jelly creep into?

....

2. What happens when she goes into the hollow log? ....

....

3. Is the big rabbit happy or cross with Jelly?..

....

....

22B activity 4

Photocopiable activities from Jelly and Bean

Name..

Use the words in the boxes to fill in the gaps in the sentences.

| string | stick | catch |

Kevin has a bent stick with a piece of .... at one end. Wellington has a long .... with a net on the end. The dogs go to the pond to .... some fish. They sit on the bank with the string and the net in the water.

Name..

Write the correct word in each space.

| string | feels | fishes |

Kevin feels a tug on the ....

Wellington .... a tug on the net.

The dogs pull up the string and the net.

Oh no! They have not got ....

They have got frogs!

Name..

Write a story about these pictures.

| stick | fishing |
| catch | frogs |

....

....

....

....

23B activity 3   Photocopiable activities from Jelly and Bean

Name..

Write the answers to the questions on the dotted lines.

1. What is Kevin doing at the pond?

....

2. What is Wellington holding in his mouth?

....

3. What do the dogs catch?

....

....

....

....

23B activity 4

Photocopiable activities from Jelly and Bean

Name..

Write the correct word in each space.

dish

choc-chips

quick

Colin is a very big cat. He has a .... as big as a hat. It is full of .... Colin eats the choc-chips very .... He is full. He feels sick.

Name..

Write the correct word in each space.

quick

stay

greedy

Colin has eaten the choc-chips too .... He feels sick. He flops down on Kevin's bed. Kevin comes to see him. 'You are a .... cat,' he says, 'but you can .... on my bed until you feel better.'

Name..

Join up each pair of rhyming words with a line.

bed	hat
cat	red
chips	Kevin
Colin	dish
wish	lips

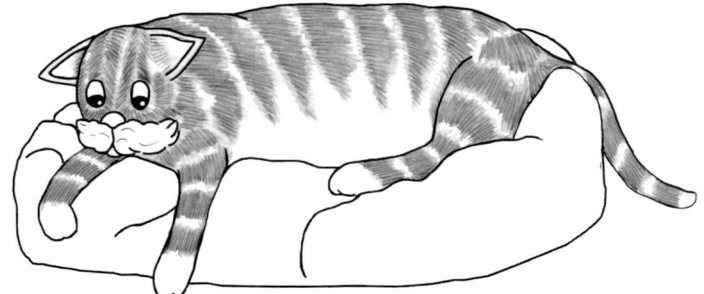

24B activity 3   Photocopiable activities from Jelly and Bean

Name..

Write the answers to the questions on the dotted lines.

1. What is in Colin's dish?

....

2. Does Colin eat too much?

....

3. How does Colin feel?

....

4. What does Kevin let him do?

....

....

....

24B activity 4

Photocopiable activities from Jelly and Bean

Name..

Can you find the words?
shell chick quick fish hatch they

Write each word next to a little chick.

s	h	e	l	l	q
f	i	s	h	w	u
h	a	t	c	h	i
z	t	h	e	y	c
c	h	i	c	k	k

Photocopiable activities from Jelly and Bean

Name..

Can you find the words?

speed down about rain good water

Write each word next to a pool of rain.

s	p	e	e	d	w
a	b	o	u	t	a
d	r	a	i	n	t
g	o	o	d	t	e
y	d	o	w	n	r

....　　..............................

....　　..............................

....　　..............................

Photocopiable activities from Jelly and Bean